At Sylvan, we believe reading is one of life's most important and enriching abilities, and we're glad you've chosen our resources to help your children build this critically important skill. We know that the time you spend with your children reinforcing the lessons learned in school will contribute to their love of reading. This love of reading will translate into academic achievement. Successful readers are ready for the world around them; they are prepared to do research, to experience literature, and to make the connections necessary to achieve in school and life.

In teaching reading at Sylvan, we use a research-based, step-by-step process, which includes thought-provoking reading selections and activities. Our Sylvan workbooks are designed to help you to help your children build the skills and confidence that will contribute to their success in school.

We're excited to partner with you to support the development of a confident, well-prepared independent learner!

The Sylvan Team

Sylvan Learning Center

Build the skills, habits, and attitudes your child needs to succeed in school and in life.

Sylvan Learning is the leading provider of tutoring and supplemental education services to students of all ages and skill levels. At Sylvan, our warm and caring tutors tailor individualized learning plans that build the skills, habits, and attitudes students need to succeed in school and in life. Affordable tutoring instruction is available in math, reading, writing, study skills, homework help, test prep, and more at more than 750 learning centers in the United States, Canada, and abroad.

The proven, personalized approach of our in-center programs delivers unparalleled results that other supplemental education services simply can't match. Your child's achievements will be seen not only in test scores and report cards but outside the classroom as well. You will see a new level of confidence in all of your child's activities and interactions.

At Sylvan, we want your child to be successful at every stage of his or her academic journey. Here's a glimpse into how our program works:

- Depending on your needs and your child's needs, we'll do an assessment to pinpoint skill gaps, strengths, and focus areas.

- We develop a customized learning plan designed to meet your child's academic goals.

- Through our method of skill mastery, your child will not only learn and master the skills in the personalized plan but he or she will be truly motivated and inspired to achieve.

- Our teachers are caring and highly qualified. We'll get to know your child and keep lessons fresh and fun.

- Every step of the way, we'll work together to evaluate your child's progress and learning goals.

To get started, simply contact your local Sylvan Learning Center to set up an appointment. And to learn more about Sylvan and our innovative in-center programs, call 1-800-EDUCATE or visit www.SylvanLearning.com.

Pre-K Beginning Letters Workbook

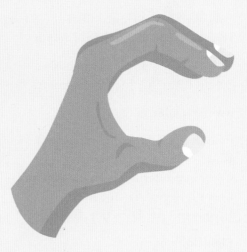

www.sylvanlearning.com

Producer & Editorial Direction: The Linguistic Edge
Writer: Margaret Crocker
Cover and Interior Illustrations: Tim Goldman, Shawn Finley, and Duendes del Sur
Cover Design: Suzanne Lee
Layout and Art Direction: SunDried Penguin

First Edition

ISBN: 978-0-307-47952-5
ISSN: 2161-9751

PRINTED IN CHINA

10 9 8 7 6 5 4 3

Contents

The Letter A

Trace & Sing

TRACE the letter **A**. START at the green arrow labeled with a number 1.

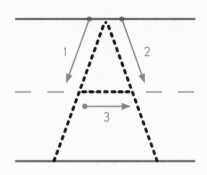

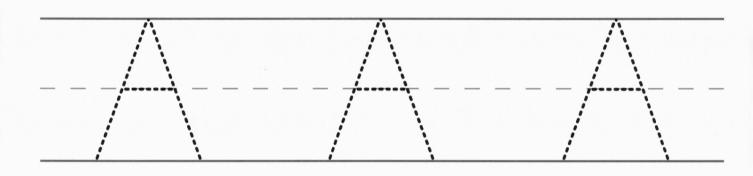

SING this song to the tune of *Wheels on the Bus*.

The letter of the day is

A-A-A, A-A-A, A-A-A!

The letter of the day is

A-A-A,

Today is letter A!

MAKE an **A** using three crayons (two long and one short).

Alphabet Art

COLOR the spaces that have the **letter of the day**. You may use any color you like.

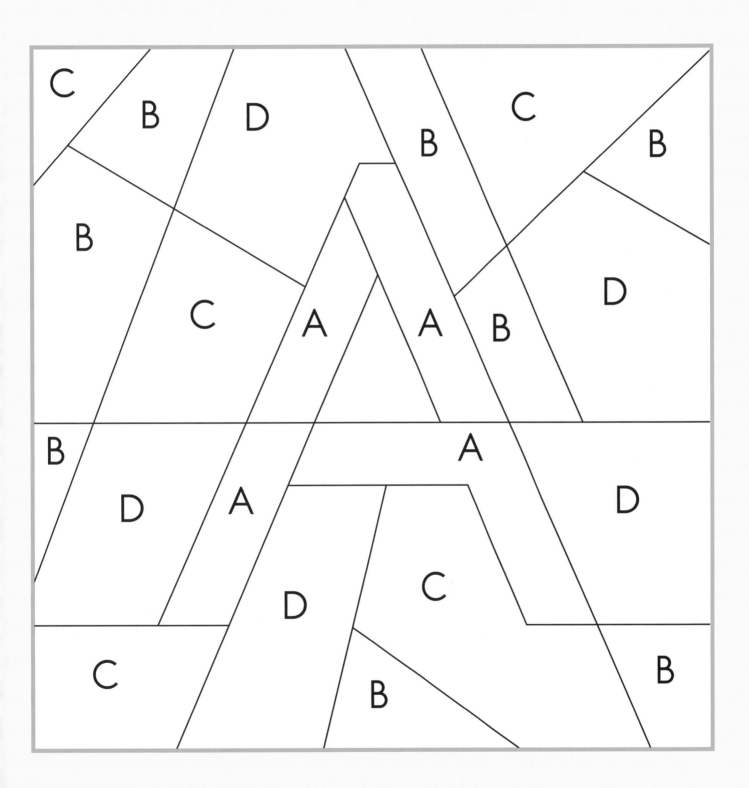

The Letter B

Trace & Sing

TRACE the letter **B**. START at the green arrow labeled with a number 1.

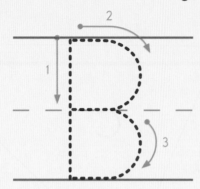

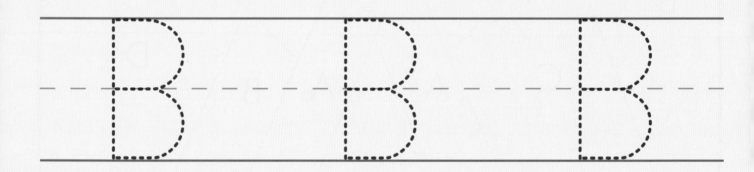

SING this song to the tune of *BINGO*.

We learn a letter every day.

Today it's letter **B**!

B, B, B-B-B!

B, B, B-B-B!

B, B, B-B-B!

And that's the letter **B**!

MAKE a **B** using beads.

Practice the Letter B

CIRCLE every **letter of the day** in the blue box.

A	B	C	D
G	R	X	B
B	O	P	F

CROSS OUT every **letter of the day** in the green box.

B	D	A	M
V	B	P	N
W	C	X	B

The Letter C

Trace & Sing

TRACE the letter C. START at the green arrow labeled with a number 1.

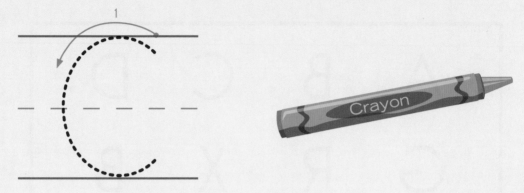

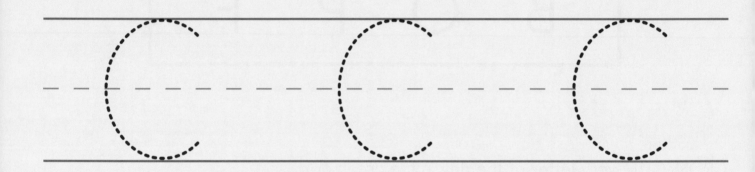

SING this song to the tune of *Wheels on the Bus*.

The letter of the day is

C-C-C, C-C-C, C-C-C!

The letter of the day is

C-C-C,

Today is letter C!

MAKE a C using your left hand.

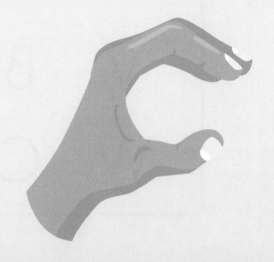

Practice the Letter C

COLOR every cat that is wearing the **letter of the day**.

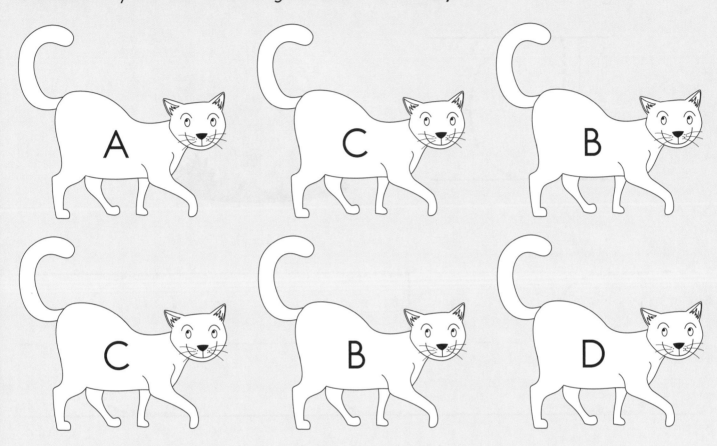

DRAW a line to connect each pair of matching letters.

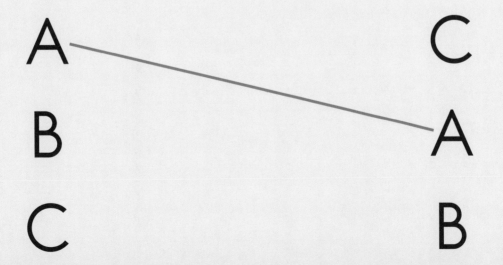

Trace & Sing

TRACE the letter **D**. START at the green arrow labeled with a number 1.

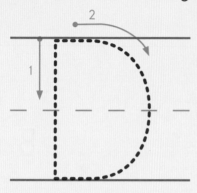

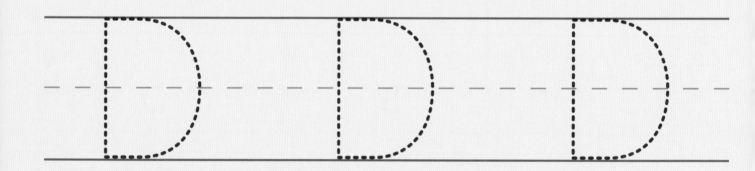

SING this song to the tune of *BINGO*.

We learn a letter every day.

Today it's letter **D**!

D, D, D-D-D!

D, D, D-D-D!

D, D, D-D-D!

And that's the letter **D**!

MAKE a **D** using a pencil and string.

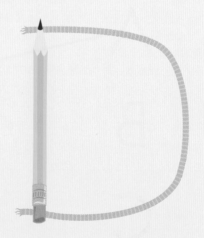

Practice the Letter D

CROSS OUT every **letter of the day** in the box.

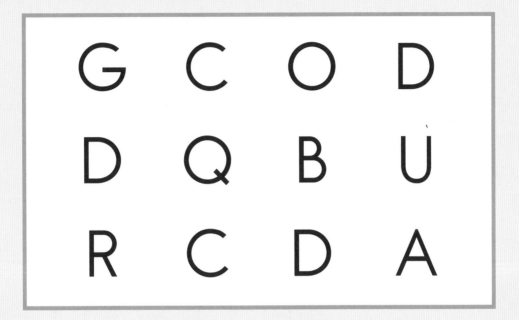

COLOR every duck wearing **D** green. COLOR every duck wearing **C** purple.

The Letter E

Trace & Sing

TRACE the letter **E**. START at the green arrow labeled with a number 1.

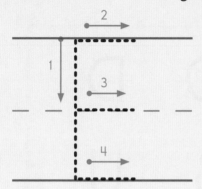

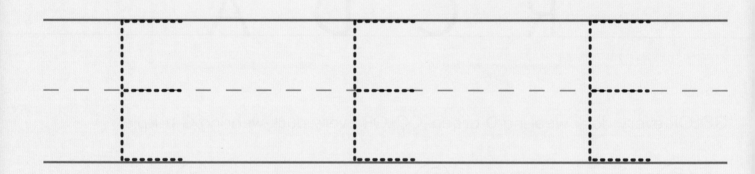

SING this song to the tune of *Wheels on the Bus*.

The letter of the day is

E-E-E, E-E-E, E-E-E!

The letter of the day is

E-E-E,

Today is letter **E**!

MAKE an **E** using four drinking straws (one long and three short).

Practice the Letter E

CIRCLE every **letter of the day** in the box.

E	F	B	D
A	B	E	H
K	P	B	E

DRAW a line to connect each pair of matching letters.

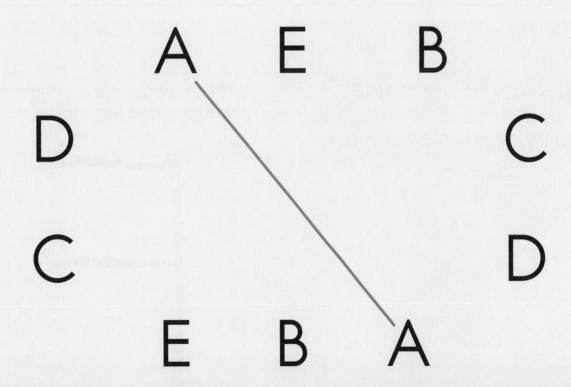

The Letter F

Trace & Sing

TRACE the letter **F**. START at the green arrow labeled with a number 1.

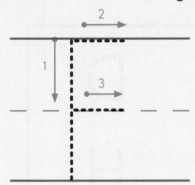

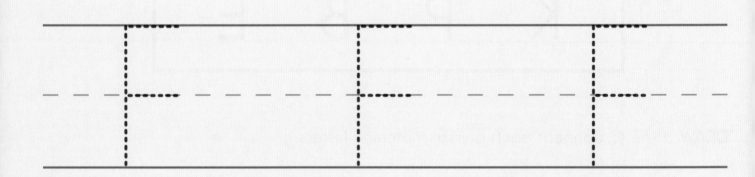

SING this song to the tune of *BINGO*.

We learn a letter every day.

Today it's letter **F**!

F, F, F-F-F!

F, F, F-F-F!

F, F, F-F-F!

And that's the letter **F**!

MAKE an **F** using three sticks (one long and two short).

Alphabet Art

COLOR the **F** spaces green. COLOR the **E** spaces red.

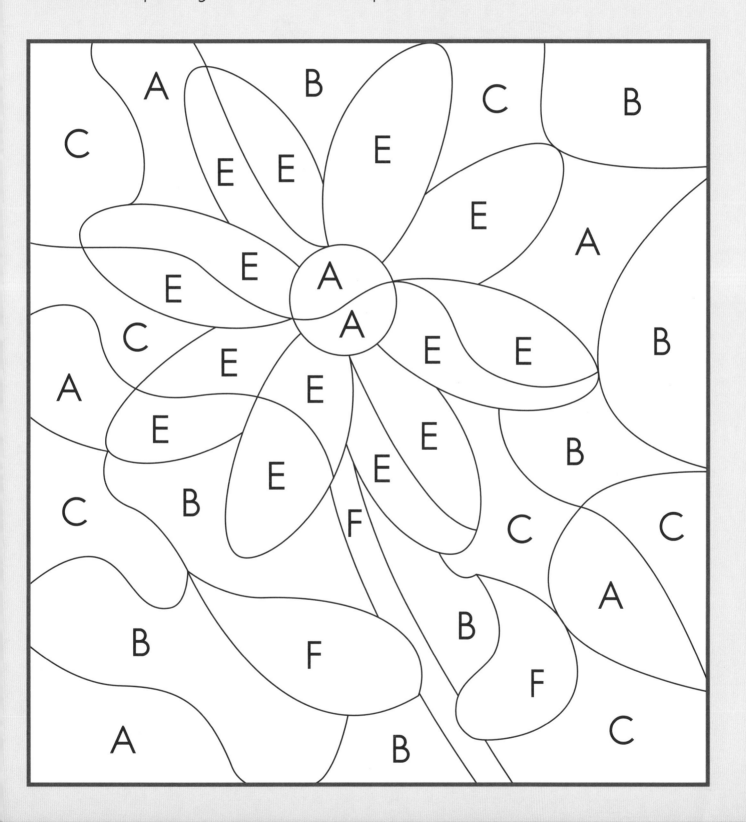

The Letter G

Trace & Sing

TRACE the letter **G**. START at the green arrow labeled with a number 1.

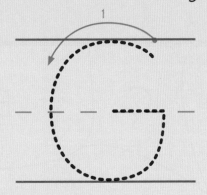

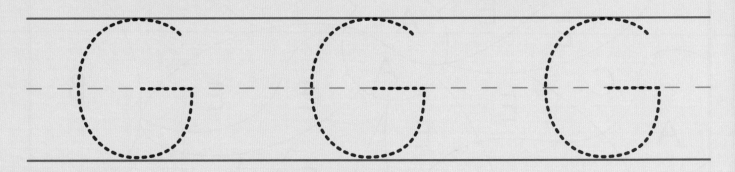

SING this song to the tune of *Wheels on the Bus.*

The letter of the day is

G-G-G, G-G-G, G-G-G!

The letter of the day is

G-G-G,

Today is letter **G!**

MAKE a **G** using clay.

Practice the Letter G

CROSS OUT every **letter of the day** in the box.

C	G	D	Q
B	O	P	G
G	R	K	X

COLOR every girl wearing **G** green. COLOR every girl wearing **B** blue.

Match Maker

DRAW a line to connect each pair of matching letters.

A	D
B	G
C	B
D	A
E	F
F	C
G	E

Trace & Color

TRACE the letters. SAY the name of each letter as you trace.

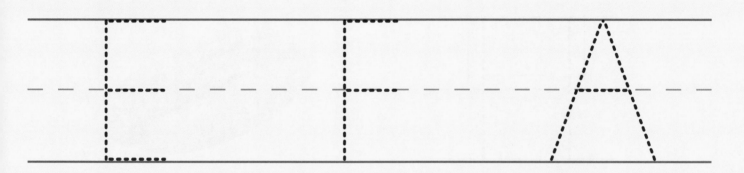

COLOR every cow wearing **B** blue. COLOR every cow wearing **D** red. Then COLOR every cow wearing **E** orange.

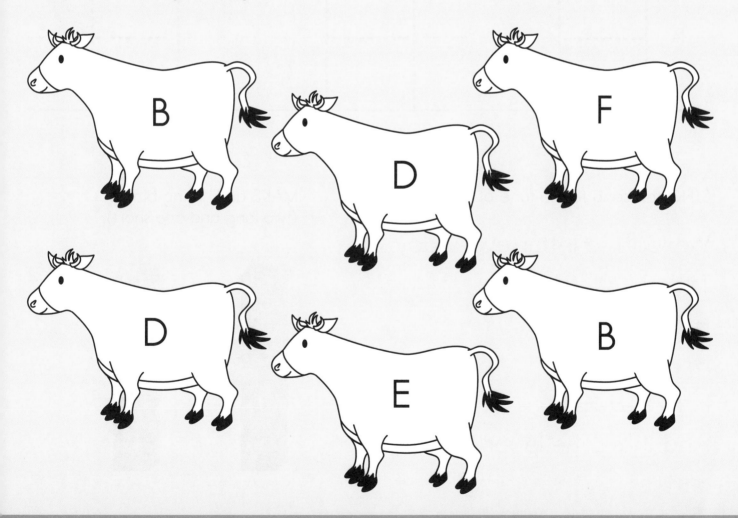

The Letter H

Trace & Sing

TRACE the letter **H**. START at the green arrow labeled with a number 1.

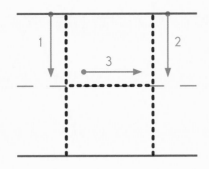

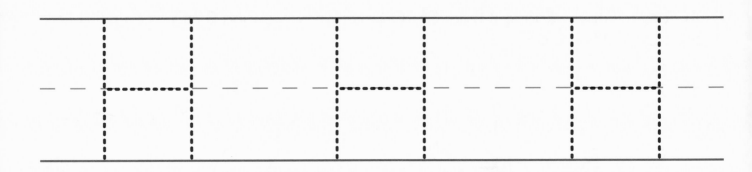

SING this song to the tune of *BINGO*.

We learn a letter every day.

Today it's letter **H**!

H, H, H-H-H!

H, H, H-H-H!

H, H, H-H-H!

And that's the letter **H**!

MAKE an **H** using blocks
(two long and one short).

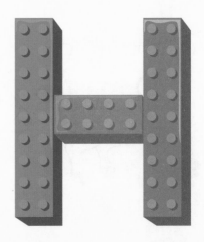

Practice the Letter H

COLOR every hat that has the **letter of the day**.

CIRCLE every **letter of the day** in the box. Then CROSS OUT every **D**.

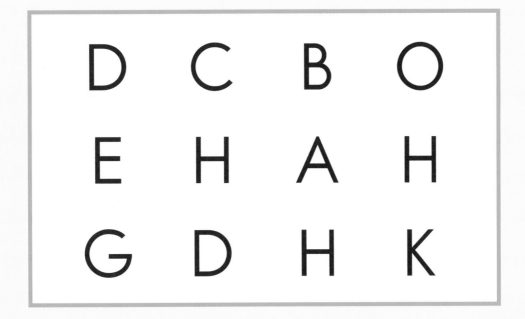

Trace & Sing

TRACE the letter **I**. START at the green arrow labeled with a number 1.

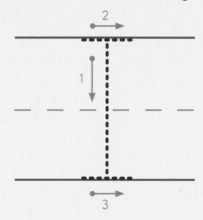

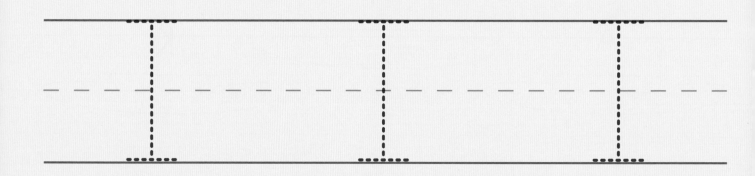

SING this song to the tune of *Wheels on the Bus*.

FIND three things that look like an **I**.

The letter of the day is

I-I-I, I-I-I, I-I-I!

The letter of the day is

I-I-I,

Today is letter **I**!

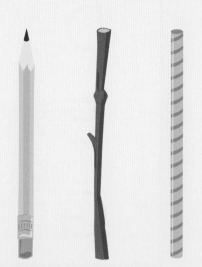

Practice the Letter I

CROSS OUT every **letter of the day** in the box.

T I J L

P V A I

I Y I T

DRAW a line to connect each pair of matching letters.

D G H I A F

E B

F D

G A I B E H

Trace & Sing

TRACE the letter **J**. START at the green arrow labeled with a number 1.

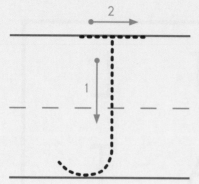

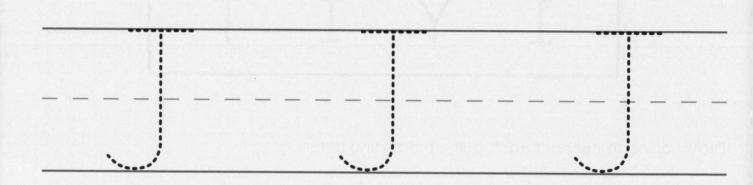

SING this song to the tune of *BINGO*.

We learn a letter every day.

Today it's letter **J**!

J, J, J-J-J!

J, J, J-J-J!

J, J, J-J-J!

And that's the letter **J**!

MAKE a **J** using a scarf.

Practice the Letter J

COLOR every jellybean that is wearing the **letter of the day**.

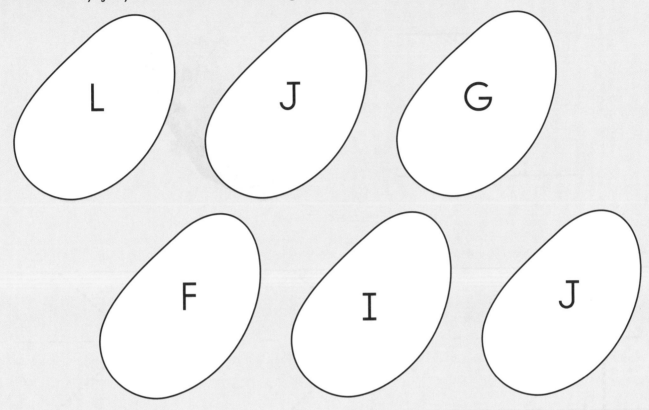

CIRCLE every **letter of the day** in the box. Then CROSS OUT every **I**.

J	L	I	K
I	U	J	L
V	I	L	J

The Letter K

Trace & Sing

TRACE the letter K. START at the green arrow labeled with a number 1.

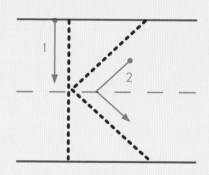

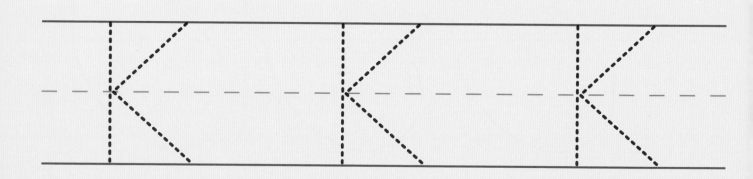

SING this song to the tune of *Wheels on the Bus.*

The letter of the day is

K-K-K, K-K-K, K-K-K!

The letter of the day is

K-K-K,

Today is letter K!

MAKE a K using green beans (one long and two short).

Practice the Letter K

CIRCLE every **letter of the day** in the box.

H	K	A	Z
K	X	W	K
R	V	K	Y

DRAW a line to connect each pair of matching letters.

D H K I G E

F   J

E   G

H K J D F I

The Letter L

Trace & Sing

TRACE the letter **L**. START at the green arrow labeled with a number 1.

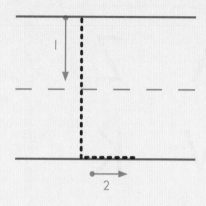

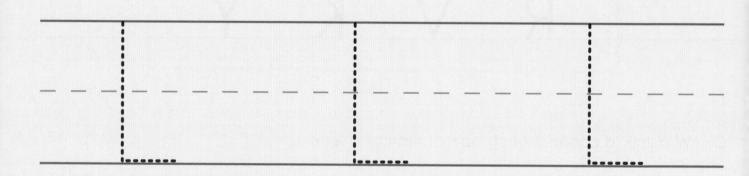

SING this song to the tune of *BINGO*.

We learn a letter every day.

Today it's letter **L**!

L, L, L-L-L!

L, L, L-L-L!

L, L, L-L-L!

And that's the letter **L**!

MAKE an **L** using your left hand.

Alphabet Art

COLOR the **L** spaces orange. COLOR the **J** spaces black. Then COLOR the **I** spaces red.

The Letter M

Trace & Sing

TRACE the letter **M**. START at the green arrow labeled with a number 1.

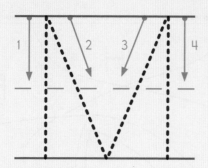

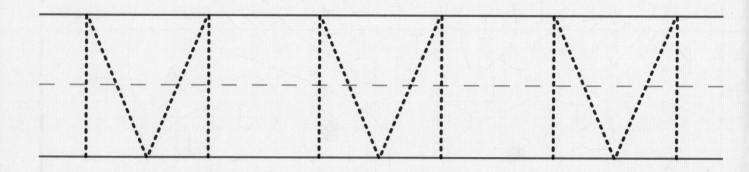

SING this song to the tune of *Wheels on the Bus*.

The letter of the day is

M-M-M, M-M-M, M-M-M!

The letter of the day is

M-M-M,

Today is letter **M**!

MAKE an **M** out of two pairs of pants.

28

Practice the Letter M

CIRCLE every **letter of the day** in the box. CROSS OUT every letter **H**.

```
N   M   H   A
K   H   W   M
H   E   M   V
```

DRAW a line to connect each pair of matching letters.

```
    K H M F
 G           J

                L
I
                H
J

 K              I
    M L F G
```

The Letter N

Trace & Sing

TRACE the letter **N**. START at the green arrow labeled with a number 1.

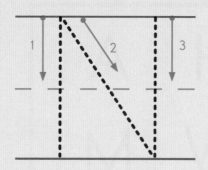

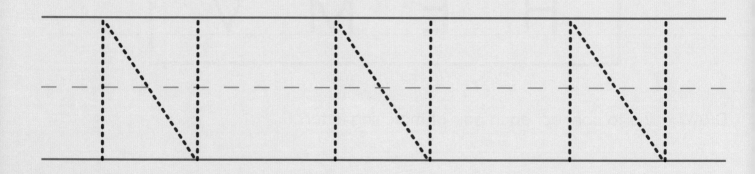

SING this song to the tune of *BINGO*.

We learn a letter every day.

Today it's letter **N**!

N, N, N-N-N!

N, N, N-N-N!

N, N, N-N-N!

And that's the letter **N**!

MAKE an **N** using three pencils.

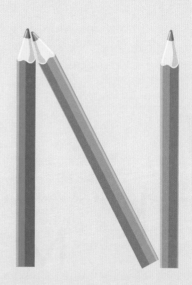

Alphabet Art

COLOR the **N** spaces brown. COLOR the **M** spaces blue. Then COLOR the **A** spaces red.

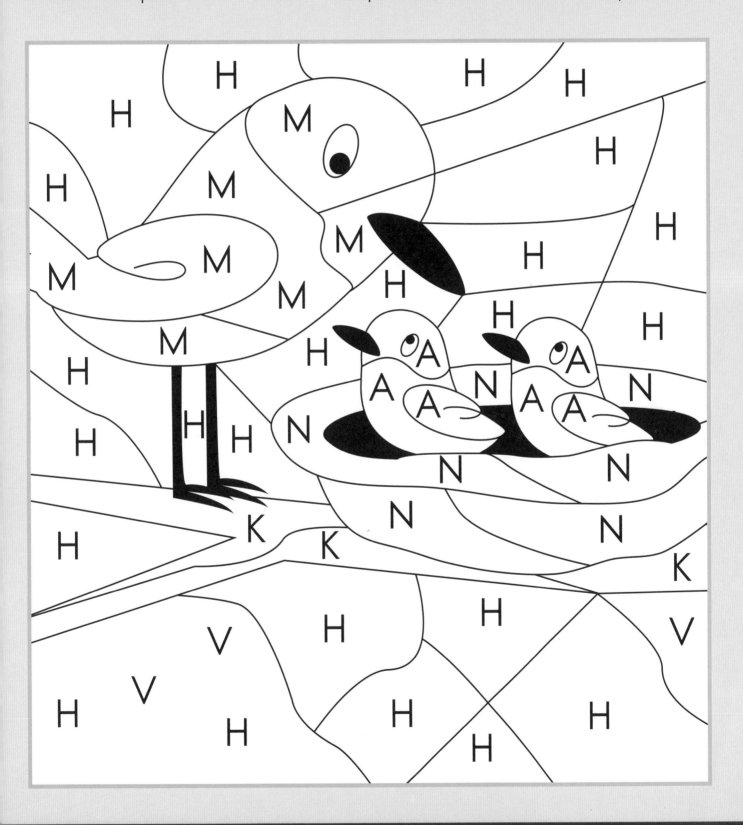

The Letter O

Trace & Sing

TRACE the letter O. START at the green arrow labeled with a number 1.

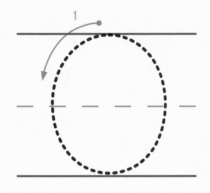

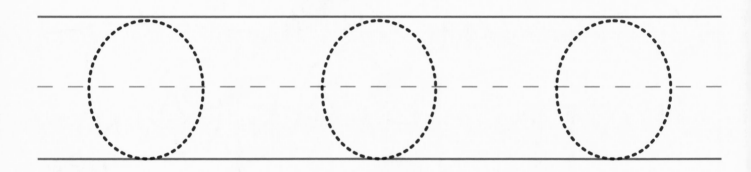

SING this song to the tune of *Wheels on the Bus.*

The letter of the day is

O-O-O, O-O-O, O-O-O!

The letter of the day is

O-O-O,

Today is letter O!

FIND three things that look like an O.

Practice the Letter O

CIRCLE every **letter of the day** in the box. CROSS OUT every letter **G**.

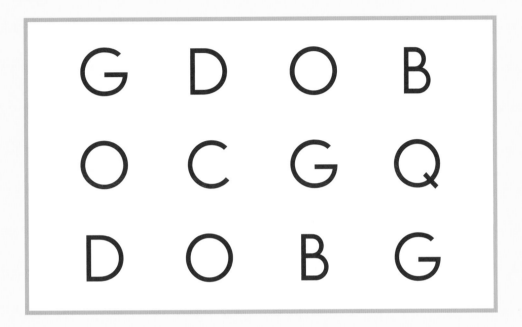

COLOR every owl wearing **O** orange. COLOR every owl wearing **D** blue. Then COLOR every owl wearing **G** green.

Trace & Sing

TRACE the letter **P**. START at the green arrow labeled with a number 1.

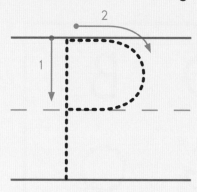

Hello Polly

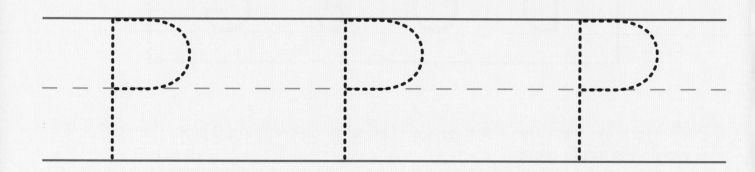

SING this song to the tune of *BINGO*.

We learn a letter every day.

Today it's letter **P**!

P, P, P-P-P!

P, P, P-P-P!

P, P, P-P-P!

And that's the letter **P**!

MAKE a **P** with two pieces of licorice.

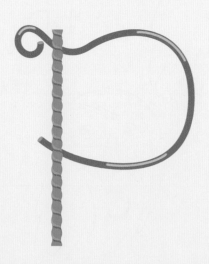

Practice the Letter P

CIRCLE every **letter of the day** in the box. CROSS OUT every letter **B**.

D	B	P	R
P	K	B	D
F	P	R	B

DRAW a line to connect each pair of matching letters.

J   I M O K   N

L   P

M   L

P   O N J I K

Match Maker

SING the alphabet song. FOLLOW ALONG with the alphabet. DRAW a line to connect each letter in the box to its place in the alphabet.

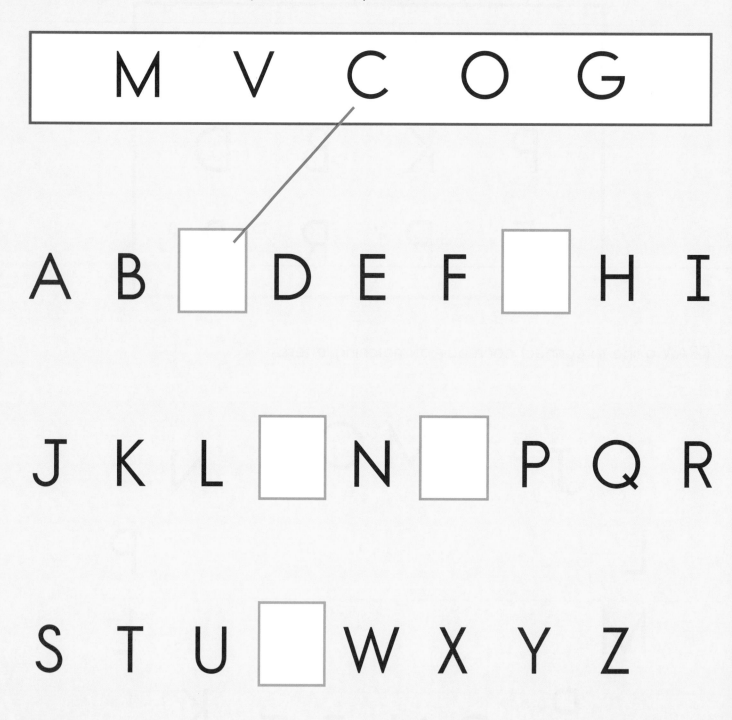

Tricky Trace

TRACE the letters. SAY the name of each letter as you trace.

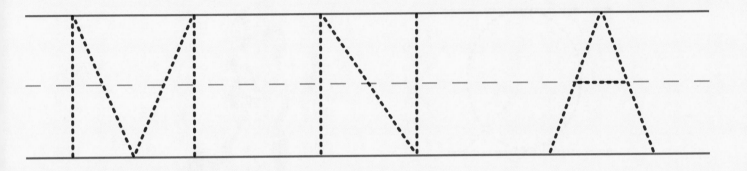

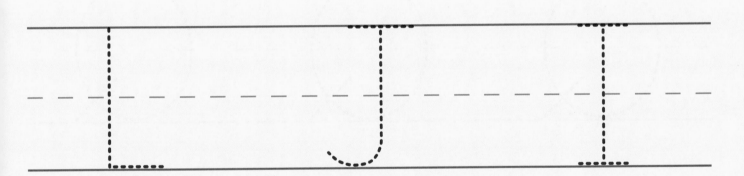

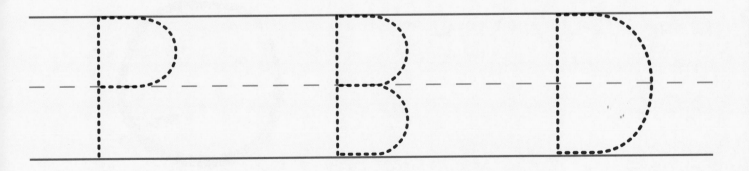

The Letter Q

Trace & Sing

TRACE the letter **Q**. START at the green arrow labeled with a number 1.

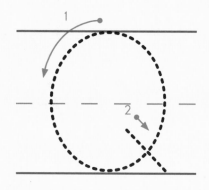

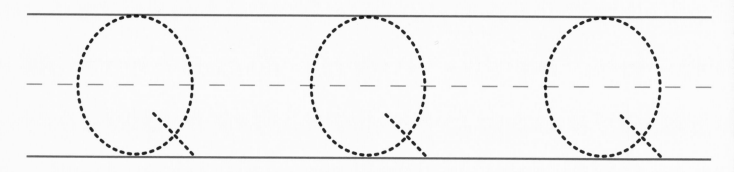

SING this song to the tune of
Wheels on the Bus.

The letter of the day is

Q-Q-Q, Q-Q-Q, Q-Q-Q!

The letter of the day is

Q-Q-Q,

Today is letter **Q**!

DRAW a **Q**. It's just a circle with a
short line crossing near the bottom.

Alphabet Art

COLOR the **Q** spaces blue. COLOR the **O** spaces green. Then COLOR the **C** spaces pink.

D	G	B	G	D
G	C C / C C	C C / O Q	C C / C C	G
B	O / C C / Q	Q O	Q / C C	B
G	C C / C C	Q O / C C	C C	G
D	G	B	G	D

The Letter R

Trace & Sing

TRACE the letter **R**. START at the green arrow labeled with a number 1.

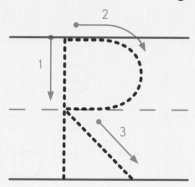

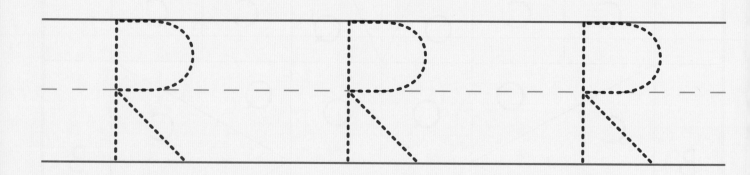

SING this song to the tune of *BINGO*.

We learn a letter every day.

Today it's letter **R**!

R, R, R-R-R!

R, R, R-R-R!

R, R, R-R-R!

And that's the letter **R**!

MAKE an **R** with ribbon and a ruler.

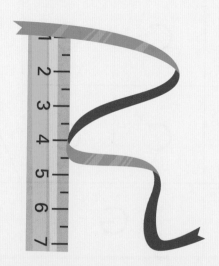

Practice the Letter R

CIRCLE every **letter of the day** in the box. CROSS OUT every letter **K**.

B	R	P	K
K	H	R	L
G	A	K	R

COLOR every robot wearing **R** red. COLOR every robot wearing **P** purple. Then COLOR every robot wearing **B** blue.

Trace & Sing

TRACE the letter S. START at the green arrow labeled with a number 1.

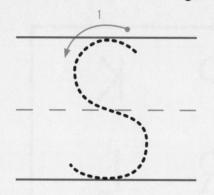

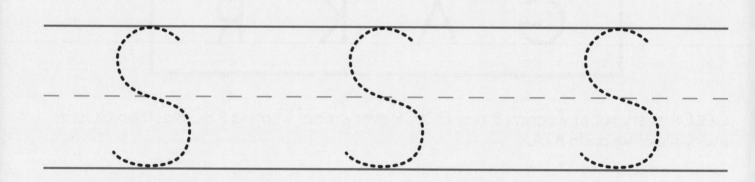

SING this song to the tune of *Wheels on the Bus*.

The letter of the day is

S-S-S, S-S-S, S-S-S!

The letter of the day is

S-S-S,

Today is letter **S**!

MAKE an **S** out of string.

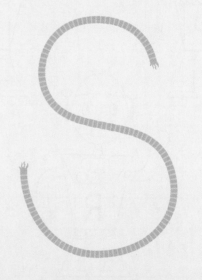

Practice the Letter S

CIRCLE every **letter of the day** in the box.

C	S	G	R
S	Z	Q	S
P	U	S	W

DRAW a line to connect each pair of matching letters.

M L P Q N S

O   M

L   R

N Q S R O P

The Letter T

Trace & Sing

TRACE the letter **T**. START at the green arrow labeled with a number 1.

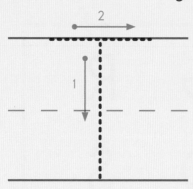

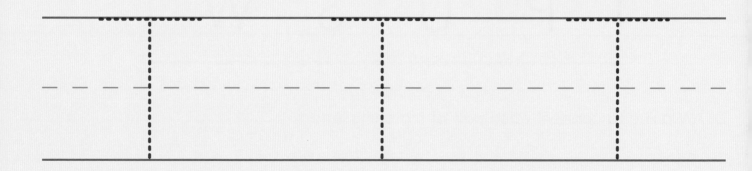

SING this song to the tune of *BINGO*.

We learn a letter every day.

Today it's letter **T**!

T, T, T-T-T!

T, T, T-T-T!

T, T, T-T-T!

And that's the letter **T**!

MAKE a **T** with two twigs
(one long and one short).

Practice the Letter T

CROSS OUT every **letter of the day** in the box.

```
I   F   T   K

E   T   A   T

L   H   T   I
```

COLOR every turkey wearing **T** brown. COLOR every turkey wearing **I** pink. Then COLOR every turkey wearing **F** yellow.

The Letter U

Trace & Sing

TRACE the letter **U**. START at the green arrow labeled with a number 1.

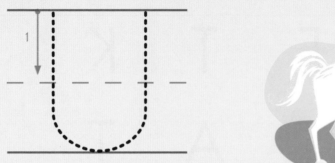

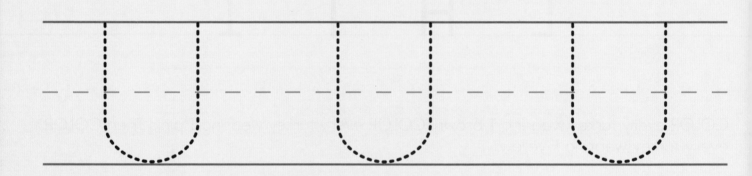

SING this song to the tune of
Wheels on the Bus.

The letter of the day is
U-U-U, U-U-U, U-U-U!
The letter of the day is
U-U-U,
Today is letter **U**!

MAKE a **U** out of yarn.

Practice the Letter U

CIRCLE every **letter of the day** in the box. CROSS OUT every letter **O**.

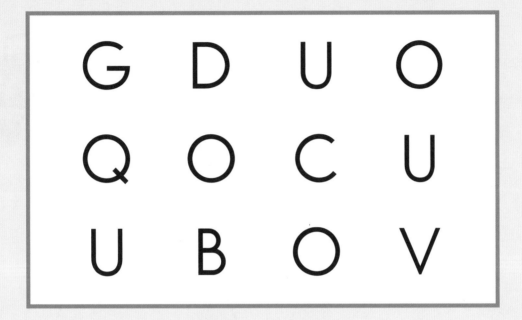

DRAW a line to connect each pair of matching letters.

T P Q U N O

R N

S S

Q U T R O P

The Letter V

Trace & Sing

TRACE the letter **V**. START at the green arrow labeled with a number 1.

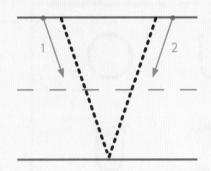

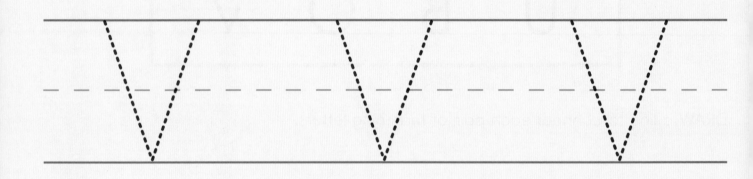

SING this song to the tune of *BINGO*.

We learn a letter every day.

Today it's letter **V**!

V, V, V-V-V!

V, V, V-V-V!

V, V, V-V-V!

And that's the letter **V**!

MAKE a **V** with your fingers.

Practice the Letter V

CROSS OUT every **letter of the day** in the box.

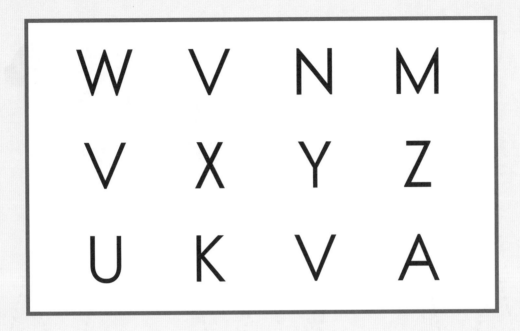

W	V	N	M
V	X	Y	Z
U	K	V	A

COLOR every van that has **V** violet. COLOR every van that has **N** green. Then COLOR every van that has **M** black.

The Letter W

Trace & Sing

TRACE the letter **W**. START at the green arrow labeled with a number 1.

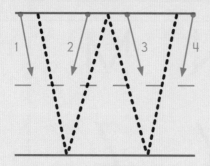

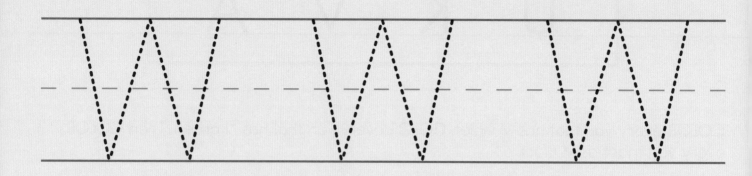

SING this song to the tune of *Wheels on the Bus*.

The letter of the day is

W (dou-ble-you), **W**, **W**!

The letter of the day is **W**,

Today is **W**!

MAKE a **W** using two pairs of jeans.

Practice the Letter W

CIRCLE every **letter of the day** in the box. CROSS OUT every letter V.

```
N   W   M   V

V   Y   M   W

W   X   V   I
```

DRAW a line to connect each pair of matching letters.

```
        V   R   Q   W
    S                   U

  T                         P

  P                         T

    W   Q   V   S   R   U
```

The Letter X

Trace & Sing

TRACE the letter **X**. START at the green arrow labeled with a number 1.

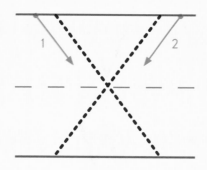

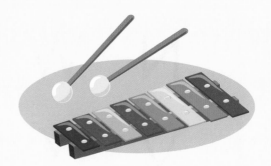

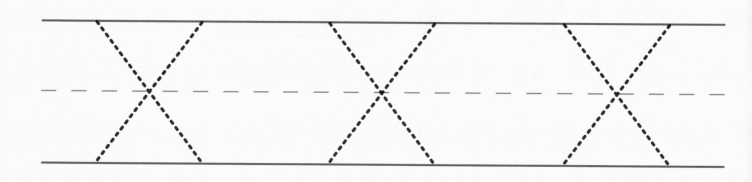

SING this song to the tune of *BINGO*.

We learn a letter every day.

Today it's letter **X**!

X, X, X-X-X!

X, X, X-X-X!

X, X, X-X-X!

And that's the letter **X**!

MAKE an **X** with two carrot sticks.

Alphabet Art

COLOR the **X** spaces blue. COLOR the **W** spaces purple. Then COLOR the **V** spaces black.

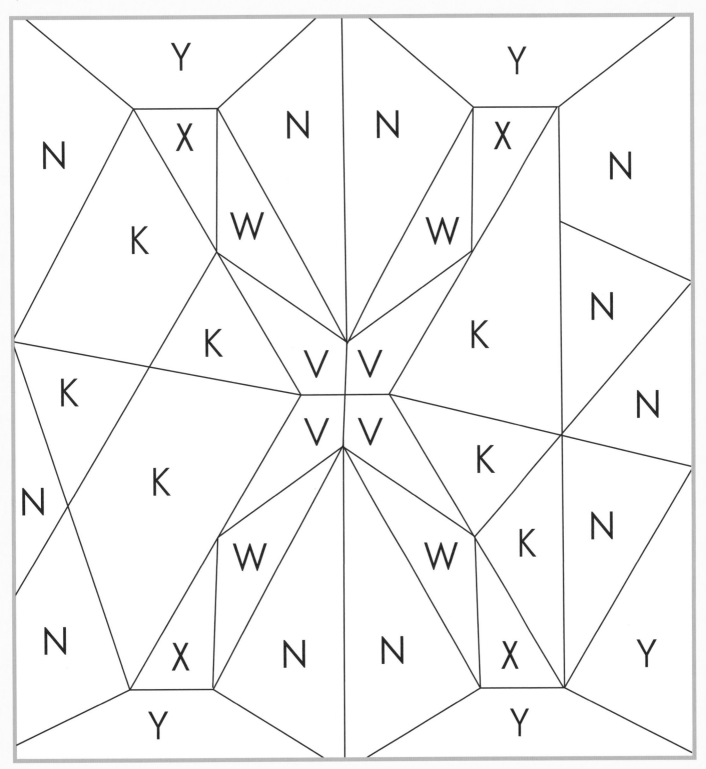

Trace & Sing

TRACE the letter **Y**. START at the green arrow labeled with a number 1.

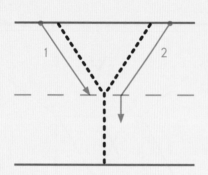

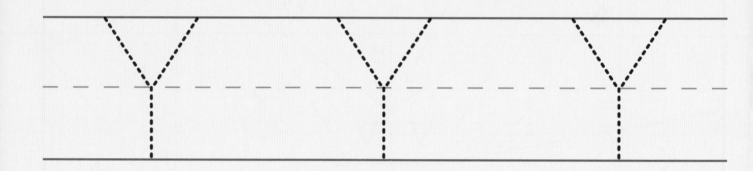

SING this song to the tune of *Wheels on the Bus*.

The letter of the day is
Y-Y-Y, Y-Y-Y, Y-Y-Y!
The letter of the day is
Y-Y-Y,
Today is letter **Y!**

MAKE a **Y** using three crayons.

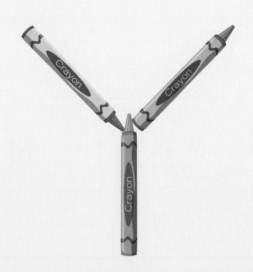

Practice the Letter Y

CIRCLE every **letter of the day** in the box.

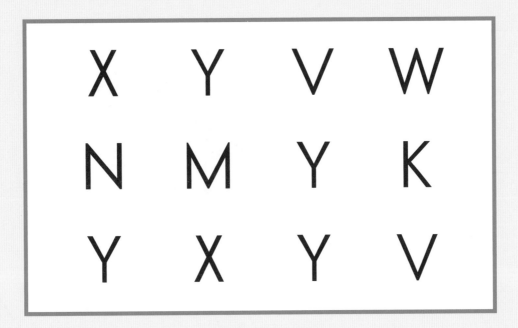

COLOR every yo-yo that has **Y** yellow. COLOR every yo-yo that has **V** green. Then COLOR every yo-yo that has **W** purple.

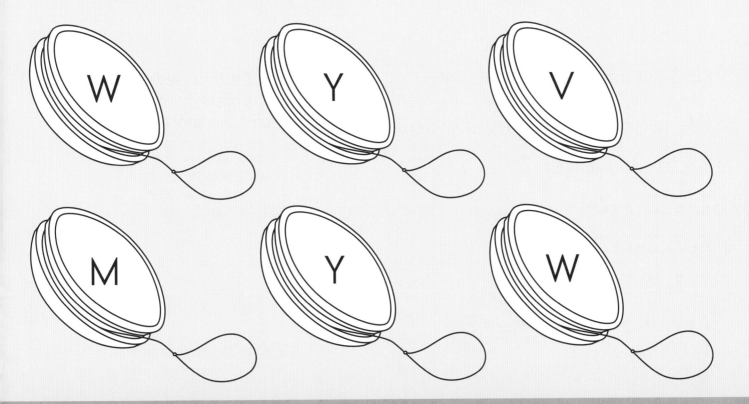

The Letter Z

Trace & Sing

TRACE the letter **Z**. START at the green arrow labeled with a number 1.

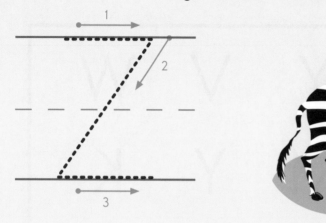

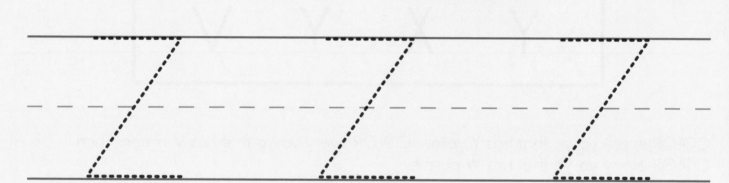

SING this song to the tune of *BINGO*.

We learn a letter every day.

Today it's letter **Z**!

Z, Z, Z-Z-Z!

Z, Z, Z-Z-Z!

Z, Z, Z-Z-Z!

And that's the letter **Z**!

MAKE a **Z** with a piece of dry spaghetti. Break it into one long piece and two short pieces.

Practice the Letter Z

CIRCLE every **letter of the day** in the box. CROSS OUT every letter **N**.

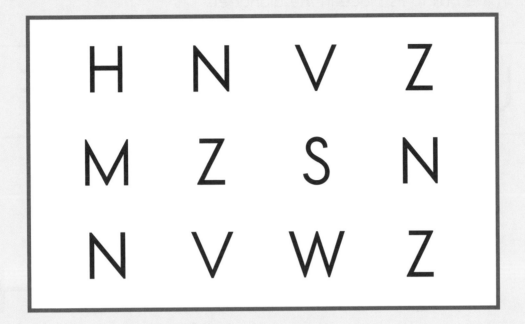

TRACE the letters. SAY the name of each letter as you trace.

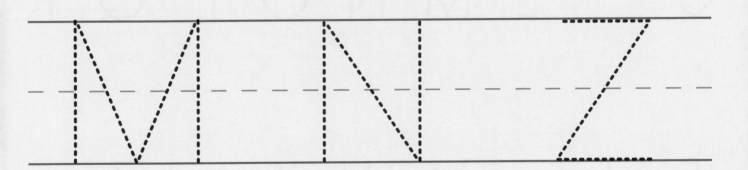

Match Maker

SING the alphabet song. FOLLOW ALONG with the alphabet. DRAW a line to connect each letter in the box to its place in the alphabet.

U K B Y F

A □ C D E □ G H I

J □ L M N O P Q R

S T □ V W X □ Z

Connect the Dots

DRAW a line to connect the dots in order from **A** to **Z**.

The Letter a

Trace & Sing

You've learned all of the uppercase ABCs! Now it's time for the lowercase abc's. Each uppercase letter has a matching lowercase letter.

Lowercase **a** matches uppercase **A**. TRACE the letter **a**. START at the green arrow labeled with a number 1.

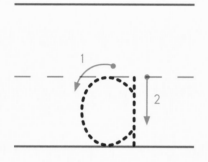

SING this song to the tune of *Jingle Bells.*

MAKE an **a** with two pieces of aluminum foil, twisted up.

Letter **a**! Letter **a**!

Hello, letter **a**!

We meet a letter every day.

Today it's letter **a**!

[Shout] **a**!

Practice the Letter a

CIRCLE every **a** in the box. CROSS OUT every **A**.

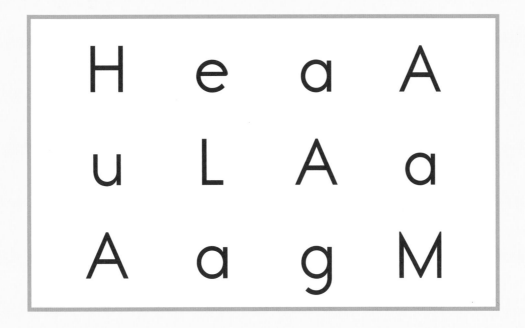

H e a A
u L A a
A a g M

COLOR every airplane that has **a** orange. COLOR every airplane that has **A** red.

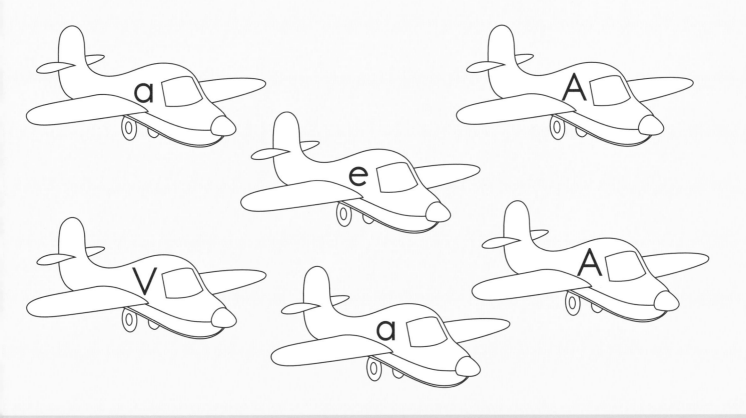

The Letter b

Trace & Sing

Lowercase **b** matches uppercase **B**. TRACE the letter **b**.
START at the green arrow labeled with a number 1.

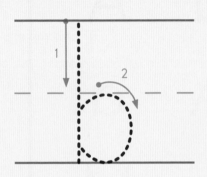

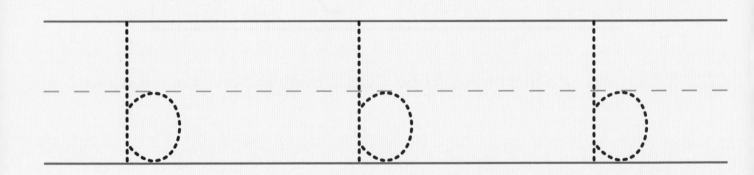

SING this song to the tune of
Mary Had a Little Lamb.

The letter of the day is **b**!

b-b-b!

b-b-b!

The letter of the day is **b**!

Today it's letter **b**!

MAKE a **b** using your favorite cereal.

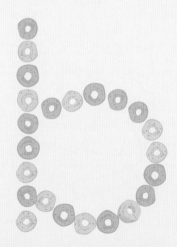

Practice the Letter b

COLOR every butterfly wearing **b** blue. COLOR every butterfly wearing **B** brown.

CIRCLE every **b** in the box. CROSS OUT every **B**.

G	B	H	b
d	b	h	B
B	D	b	p

Trace & Sing

Lowercase **c** matches uppercase **C**. TRACE the letter **c**. START at the green arrow labeled with a number 1.

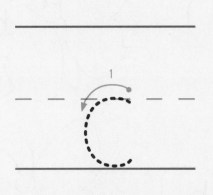

SING this song to the tune of *Jingle Bells*.

DRAW a **c** on the sidewalk with chalk.

Letter **c**! Letter **c**!

Hello, letter **c**!

We meet a letter every day.

Today it's letter **c**!

[Shout] **c**!

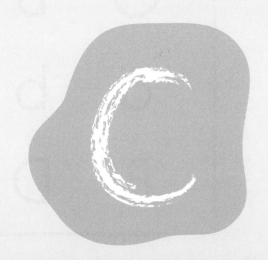

Practice the Letter c

CIRCLE every **c** in the box. CROSS OUT every **C**.

D   C   o   c

u   c   G   C

c   a   o   C

DRAW a line to connect each pair of uppercase and lowercase letters.

a   C

b   A

c   B

Trace & Sing

Lowercase **d** matches uppercase **D**. TRACE the letter **d**. START at the green arrow labeled with a number 1.

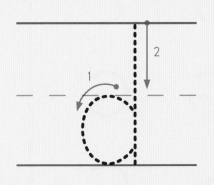

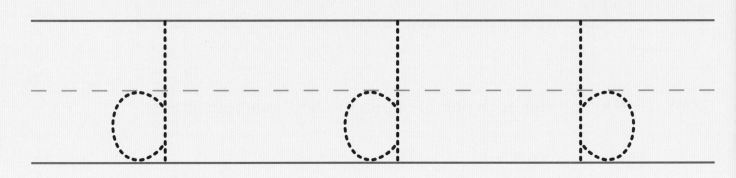

SING this song to the tune of *Mary Had a Little Lamb*.

The letter of the day is **d**!

d-d-d!

d-d-d!

The letter of the day is **d**!

Today it's letter **d**!

MAKE a **d** using your hands. Hold your right hand straight, and make a **c** with the other hand.

Practice the Letter d

COLOR every dog wearing **d** yellow. COLOR every dog wearing **D** orange. Then COLOR every dog wearing **b** red.

CIRCLE every **d** in the box. CROSS OUT every **b**.

h	d	b	j
g	b	p	d
d	h	q	b

The Letter e

Trace & Sing

Lowercase **e** matches uppercase **E**. TRACE the letter **e**. START at the green arrow labeled with a number 1.

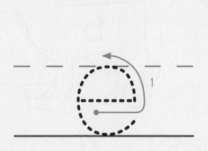

SING this song to the tune of *Jingle Bells*.

MAKE an **e** using string.

Letter **e**! Letter **e**!

Hello, letter **e**!

We meet a letter every day.

Today it's letter **e**!

[Shout] **e**!

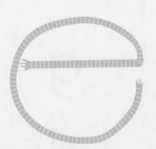

Practice the Letter e

CIRCLE every **e** in the box. CROSS OUT every **a**.

```
a   e   c   g

u   a   q   e

p   z   e   a
```

DRAW a line to connect each pair of uppercase and lowercase letters.

d   e   B

C   a

D   b

A   c   E

The Letter f

Trace & Sing

Lowercase **f** matches uppercase **F**. TRACE the letter **f**.
START at the green arrow labeled with a number 1.

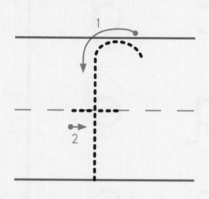

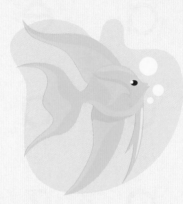

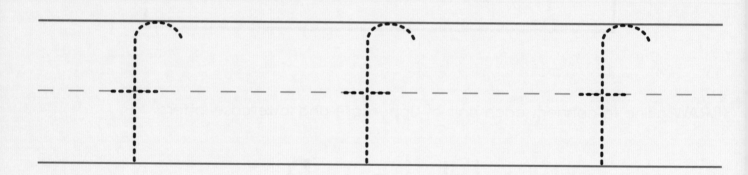

SING this song to the tune of
Mary Had a Little Lamb.

The letter of the day is **f**!

f-**f**-**f**!

f-**f**-**f**!

The letter of the day is **f**!

Today it's letter **f**!

MAKE an **f** using fish crackers.

Practice the Letter f

COLOR every fish wearing f purple. COLOR every fish wearing F blue.

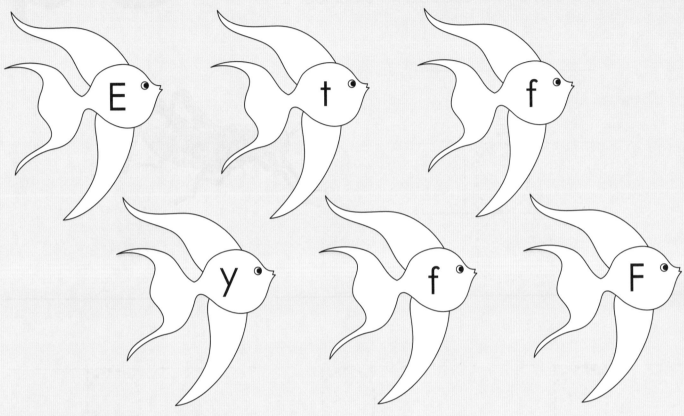

CIRCLE every f in the box.

y	h	t	f
l	f	k	t
f	t	i	f

Trace & Sing

Lowercase **g** matches uppercase **G**. TRACE the letter **g**.
START at the green arrow labeled with a number 1.

Gg

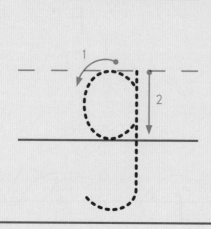

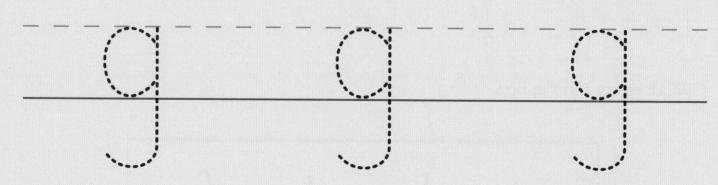

SING this song to the tune of
Jingle Bells.

MAKE a **g** using grapes.

Letter **g**! Letter **g**!

Hello, letter **g**!

We meet a letter every day.

Today it's letter **g**!

[Shout] **g**!

Alphabet Art

COLOR the **g** spaces purple. COLOR the **G** spaces green. Then COLOR the **b** spaces pink.

Match Maker

DRAW a line to connect each pair of uppercase and lowercase letters.

a	F
b	E
c	G
d	A
e	D
f	C
g	B

Trace & Color

TRACE the letters. SAY the name of each letter as you trace.

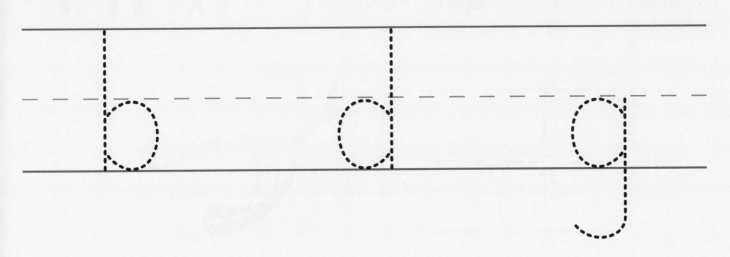

COLOR every gorilla wearing **a** orange. COLOR every gorilla wearing **c** red. Then COLOR every gorilla wearing **e** green.

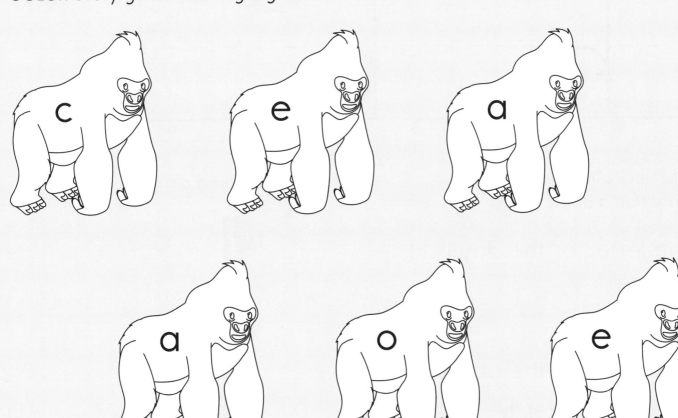

The Letter h

Trace & Sing

Lowercase **h** matches uppercase **H**. TRACE the letter **h**.
START at the green arrow labeled with a number 1.

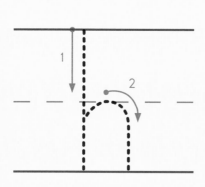

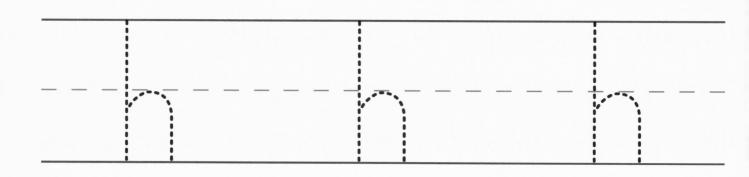

SING this song to the tune of
Mary Had a Little Lamb.

MAKE an **h** using a ruler and a sock.

The letter of the day is **h**!

h-h-h!

h-h-h!

The letter of the day is **h**!

Today it's letter **h**!

Practice the Letter h

CIRCLE every **h** in the box. CROSS OUT every **b**.

b	h	f	y
h	g	d	b
f	b	y	h

DRAW a line to connect each pair of uppercase and lowercase letters.

B a H e c d

C g

F f

E b G A D h

Trace & Sing

Lowercase **i** matches uppercase **I**. TRACE the letter **i**.
START at the green arrow labeled with a number 1.

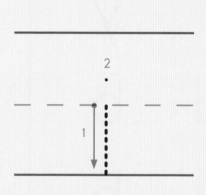

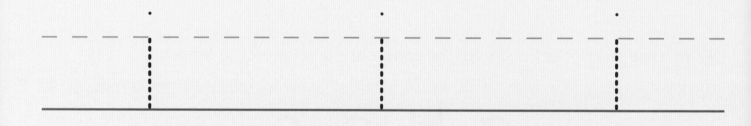

SING this song to the tune of *Jingle Bells.*

MAKE an **i** using a baby carrot and a grape.

Letter **i**! Letter **i**!

Hello, letter **i**!

We meet a letter every day.

Today it's letter **i**!

[Shout] **i**!

Practice the Letter i

COLOR every igloo that has i orange. COLOR every igloo that has **I** purple.

  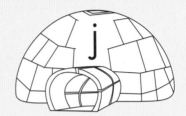

 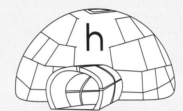 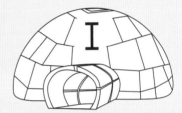

CIRCLE every i in the box.

j	i	h	t
y	r	i	d
i	t	i	j

J j

Trace & Sing

Lowercase j matches uppercase **J**. TRACE the letter **j**.
START at the green arrow labeled with a number 1.

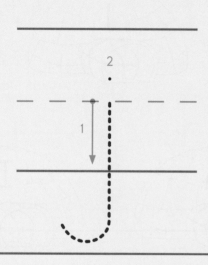

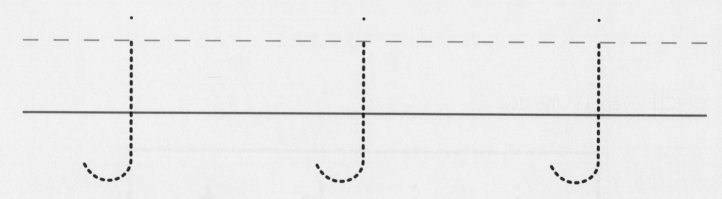

SING this song to the tune of
Mary Had a Little Lamb.

MAKE a **j** using jellybeans.

The letter of the day is **j**!

j-j-j!

j-j-j!

The letter of the day is **j**!

Today it's letter **j**!

Practice the Letter j

CIRCLE every j in the box. CROSS OUT every i.

i	j	l	t
h	t	j	i
i	l	I	j

DRAW a line to connect each pair of uppercase and lowercase letters.

f h i g d j

D C

e E

I c F G H J

Trace & Sing

Lowercase **k** matches uppercase **K**. TRACE the letter **k**.
START at the green arrow labeled with a number 1.

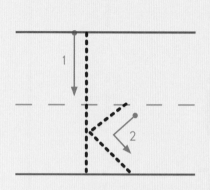

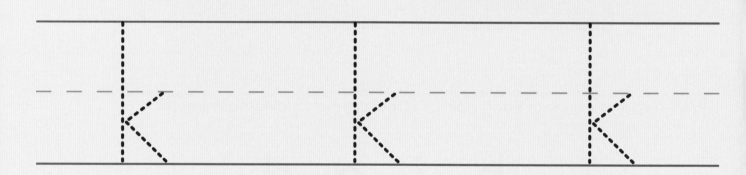

SING this song to the tune of
Jingle Bells.

MAKE a **k** using three pieces of chalk
(one long and two short).

Letter **k**! Letter **k**!

Hello, letter **k**!

We meet a letter every day.

Today it's letter **k**!

[Shout] **k**!

Practice the Letter k

CIRCLE every **k** in the box. CROSS OUT every **K**.

h	R	K	k
x	k	Y	K
K	X	k	y

COLOR every kitten wearing **k** pink. COLOR every kitten wearing **f** yellow.
Then COLOR every kitten wearing **h** green.

Trace & Sing

Lowercase **l** matches uppercase **L**. TRACE the letter l.
START at the green arrow labeled with a number 1.

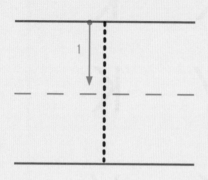

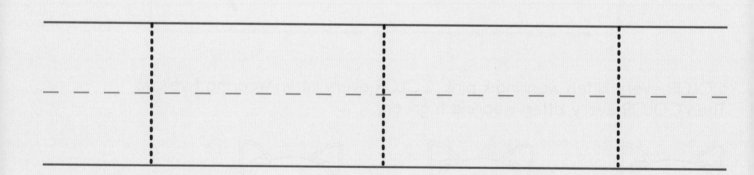

SING this song to the tune of *Mary Had a Little Lamb.*

The letter of the day is l!

l-l-l!

l-l-l!

The letter of the day is l!

Today it's letter l!

DRAW an l with your largest crayon. It's just a straight line!

Practice the Letter I

CIRCLE every **I** in the box. CROSS OUT every **L**.

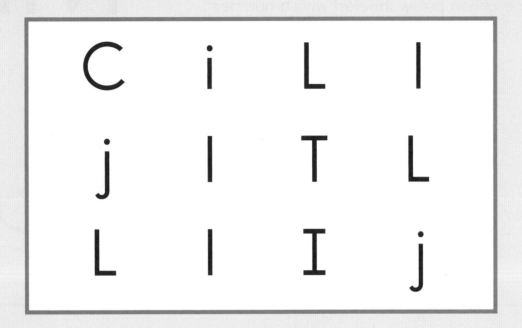

COLOR every lion wearing **I** brown. COLOR every lion wearing **i** green. Then COLOR every lion wearing **j** red.

The Letter m

Trace & Sing

Lowercase **m** matches uppercase **M**. TRACE the letter **m**.
START at the green arrow labeled with a number 1.

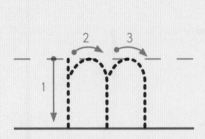

SING this song to the tune of *Jingle Bells*.

Letter **m**! Letter **m**!

Hello, letter **m**!

We meet a letter every day.

Today it's letter **m**!

[Shout] **m**!

MAKE an **m** using beads.

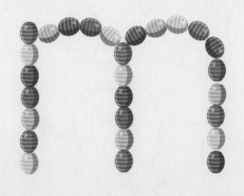

Practice the Letter m

CIRCLE every **m** in the box. CROSS OUT every **M**.

```
n    m    N    M

W    M    m    w

h    u    m    r
```

DRAW a line to connect each pair of uppercase and lowercase letters.

```
        j    i    L    k    m         g

    f                                     h

    H                                         I

        l    K    J    F    G    M
```

Trace & Sing

Lowercase **n** matches uppercase **N**. TRACE the letter **n**. START at the green arrow labeled with a number 1.

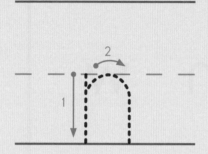

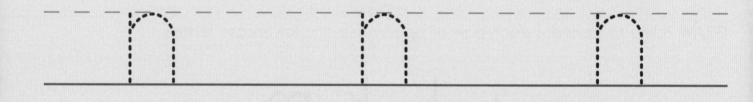

SING this song to the tune of *Mary Had a Little Lamb.*

MAKE an **n** using two pieces of spaghetti (one wet and one dry).

The letter of the day is **n**!

n-n-n!

n-n-n!

The letter of the day is **n**!

Today it's letter **n**!

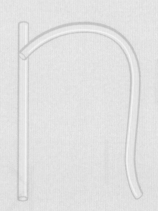

Practice the Letter n

CIRCLE every **n** in the box. CROSS OUT every **N**.

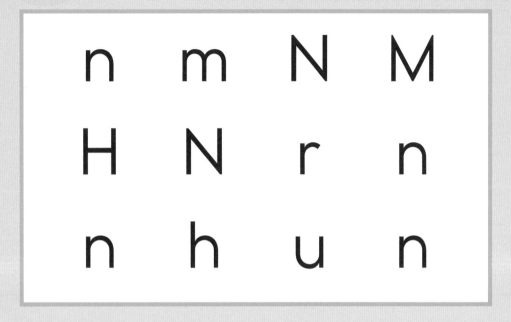

COLOR every nose wearing **n** green. COLOR every nose wearing **m** red. Then COLOR every nose wearing **h** yellow.

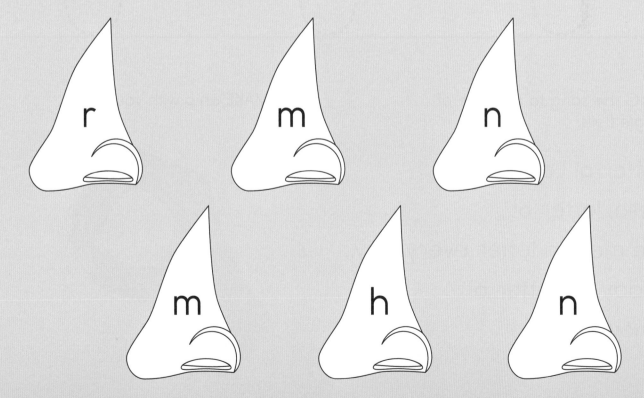

The Letter o

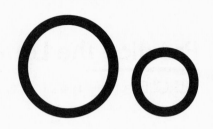

Trace & Sing

Lowercase **o** matches uppercase **O**. TRACE the letter **o**.
START at the green arrow labeled with a number 1.

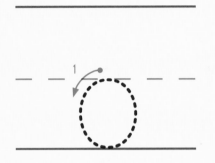

SING this song to the tune of
Jingle Bells.

Letter **o**! Letter **o**!

Hello, letter **o**!

We meet a letter every day.

Today it's letter **o**!

[Shout] **o**!

MAKE an **o** with your hand.

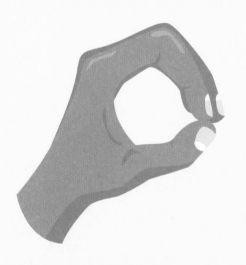

Practice the Letter o

CIRCLE every **o** in the box. CROSS OUT every **c**.

u	o	c	a
c	e	D	o
o	Q	q	c

DRAW a line to connect each pair of uppercase and lowercase letters.

O   J   B   d   E   l

m   n

D   M

b   e   L   j   N   o

The Letter p

Trace & Sing

Lowercase **p** matches uppercase **P**. TRACE the letter **p**.
START at the green arrow labeled with a number 1.

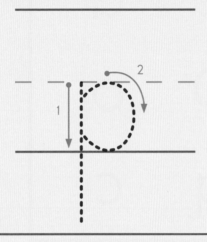

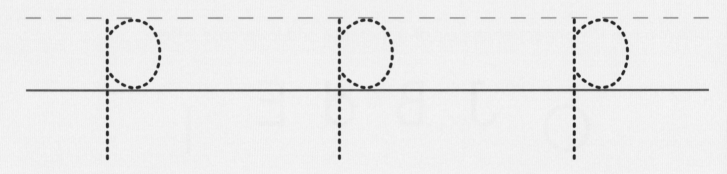

SING this song to the tune of
Mary Had a Little Lamb.

MAKE a **p** using two pillowcases.
(Take out the pillows.)

The letter of the day is **p**!

p-p-p!

p-p-p!

The letter of the day is **p**!

Today it's letter **p**!

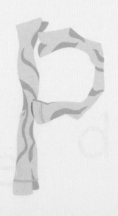

Practice the Letter p

CIRCLE every **p** in the box. CROSS OUT every **P**.

p	g	P	B
D	P	q	p
R	p	b	p

COLOR every pig wearing a **lowercase letter** blue. COLOR every pig wearing an **uppercase letter** yellow.

Tricky Trace

TRACE the letters. SAY the name of each letter as you trace.

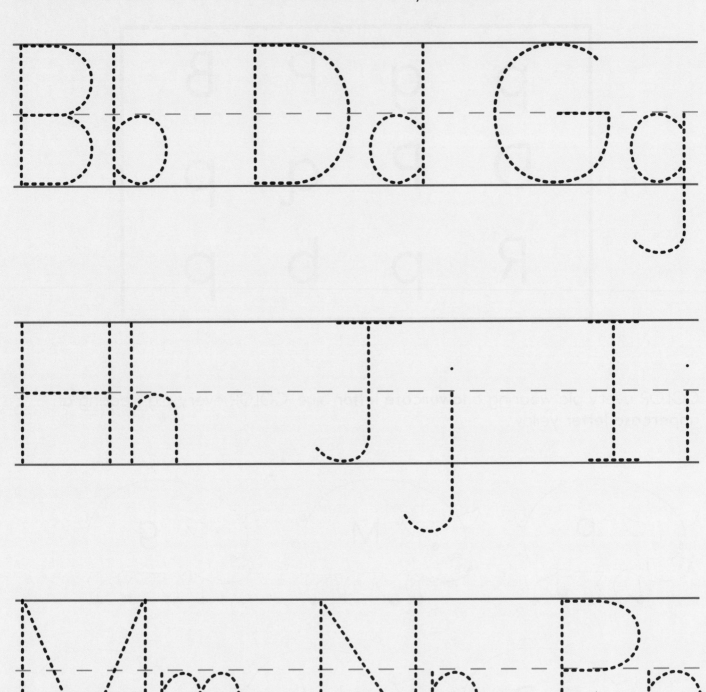

Match Maker

SING the alphabet song. FOLLOW ALONG with the alphabet. DRAW a line to connect each letter in the box to its place in the alphabet.

n   e   h   k   b

a   [ ]   c   d   [ ]   f   g   [ ]   i

j   [ ]   l   m   [ ]   o   p   q   r

s   t   u   v   w   x   y   z

The Letter q

Trace & Sing

Lowercase **q** matches uppercase **Q**. TRACE the letter **q**.
START at the green arrow labeled with a number 1.

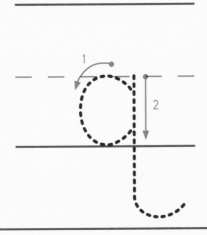

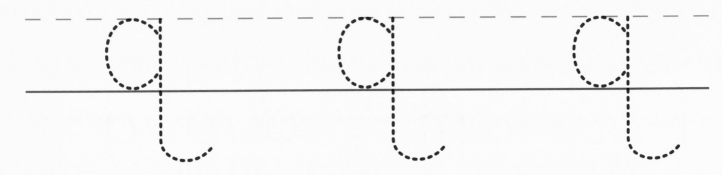

SING this song to the tune of
Jingle Bells.

Letter **q**! Letter **q**!

Hello, letter **q**!

We meet a letter every day.

Today it's letter **q**!

[Shout] **q**!

MAKE a **q** using quarters.

Practice the Letter q

CIRCLE every **q** in the box. CROSS OUT every **g**.

g	d	q	y
b	h	g	q
q	g	j	p

DRAW a line to connect each pair of uppercase and lowercase letters.

F p Q a C N

o   f

q   H

A h n c P O

Trace & Sing

Lowercase **r** matches uppercase **R**. TRACE the letter **r**.
START at the green arrow labeled with a number 1.

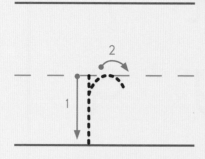

SING this song to the tune of
Mary Had a Little Lamb.

The letter of the day is **r**!

r-r-r!

r-r-r!

The letter of the day is **r**!

Today it's letter **r**!

MAKE an **r** using rocks.

Alphabet Art

COLOR the **r** spaces red. COLOR the **R** spaces green. Then COLOR the **n** spaces pink.

The Letter s

Trace & Sing

Lowercase **s** matches uppercase **S**. TRACE the letter **s**. START at the green arrow labeled with a number 1.

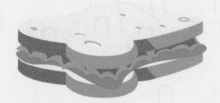

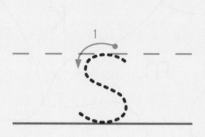

SING this song to the tune of *Jingle Bells.*

Letter **s**! Letter **s**!

Hello, letter **s**!

We meet a letter every day.

Today it's letter **s**!

[Shout] **s**!

MAKE an **s** using a shoelace.

Practice the Letter s

CIRCLE every **s** in the box. CROSS OUT every **S**.

s   z   S   Z

G   S   c   s

S   s   u   s

COLOR every snail wearing **s** purple. COLOR every snail wearing **a** yellow. Then COLOR every snail wearing **e** red.

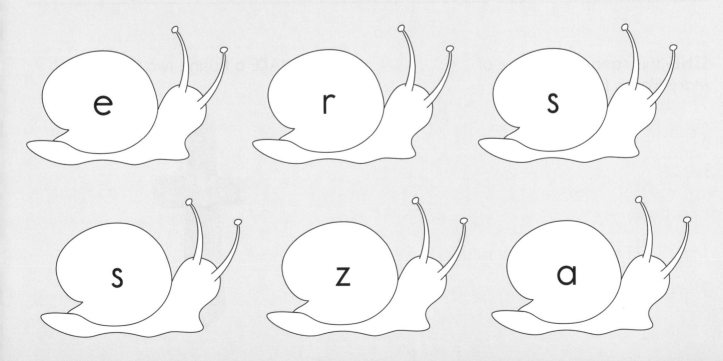

The Letter t

Trace & Sing

Lowercase **t** matches uppercase **T**. TRACE the letter **t**.
START at the green arrow labeled with a number 1.

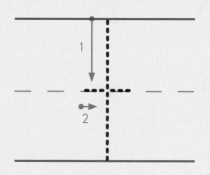

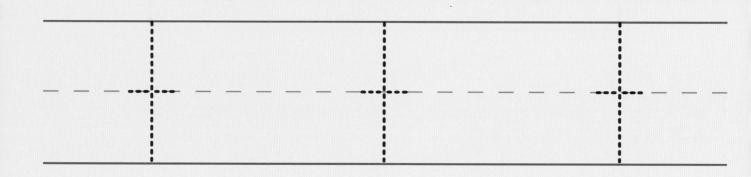

SING this song to the tune of
Mary Had a Little Lamb.

MAKE a **t** using two ties.

The letter of the day is t!

t-t-t!

t-t-t!

The letter of the day is t!

Today it's letter t!

Practice the Letter t

CIRCLE every t in the box. CROSS OUT every f.

h	f	t	k
t	b	y	f
f	t	l	t

DRAW a line to connect each pair of uppercase and lowercase letters.

r b Q T

h   c

K   S

t   H

R   q C k s   B

Trace & Sing

Lowercase **u** matches uppercase **U**. TRACE the letter **u**. START at the green arrow labeled with a number 1.

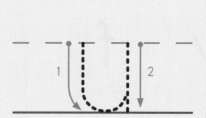

SING this song to the tune of *Jingle Bells.*

MAKE a **u** using two pieces of spaghetti (one wet and one dry).

Letter **u**! Letter **u**!

Hello, letter **u**!

We meet a letter every day.

Today it's letter **u**!

[Shout] **u**!

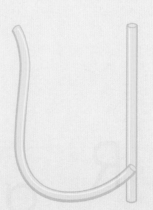

Practice the Letter u

CIRCLE every **u** in the box. CROSS OUT every **U**.

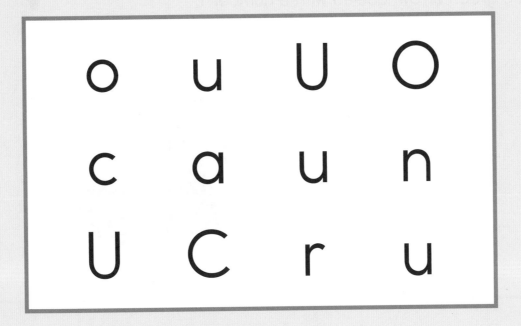

COLOR all the umbrellas with **u** purple. COLOR all the umbrellas with **n** red. Then COLOR all the umbrellas with **c** brown.

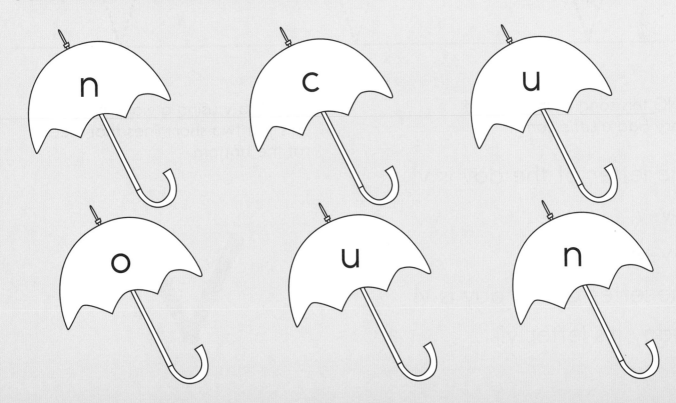

Trace & Sing

Lowercase **v** matches uppercase **V**. TRACE the letter **v**.
START at the green arrow labeled with a number 1.

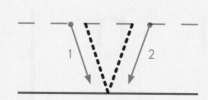

SING this song to the tune of
Mary Had a Little Lamb.

The letter of the day is **v**!

v-**v**-**v**!

v-**v**-**v**!

The letter of the day is **v**!

Today it's letter **v**!

DRAW a **v** using a violet crayon.
It's just two short lines that meet
at the bottom.

Practice the Letter v

CIRCLE every **v** in the box. CROSS OUT every **V**.

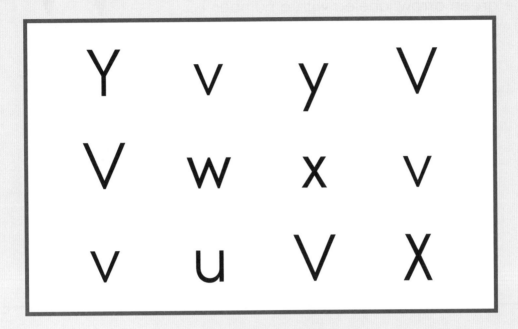

DRAW a line to connect each pair of uppercase and lowercase letters.

g v A n I T

U R

N a

r L t V u G

The Letter w

Trace & Sing

Lowercase **w** matches uppercase **W**. TRACE the letter **w**.
START at the green arrow labeled with a number 1.

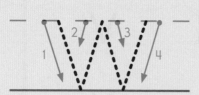

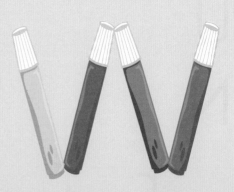

SING this song to the tune of *Jingle Bells.*

MAKE a **w** using four markers.

It's **w**, **w**!

Hello, letter **w**!

We meet a letter every day.

Today it's **w**!

[Shout] **w**!

Practice the Letter w

CIRCLE every **w** in the box. CROSS OUT every **W**.

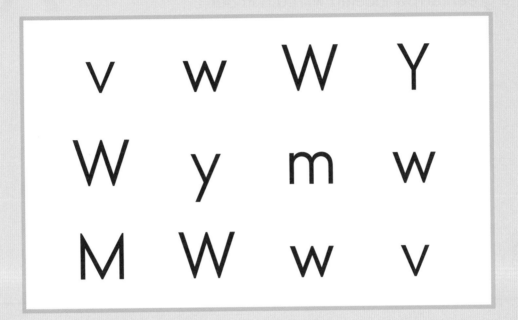

v w W Y

W y m w

M W w v

COLOR every whale wearing **w** purple. COLOR every whale wearing **u** red. Then COLOR every whale wearing **v** orange.

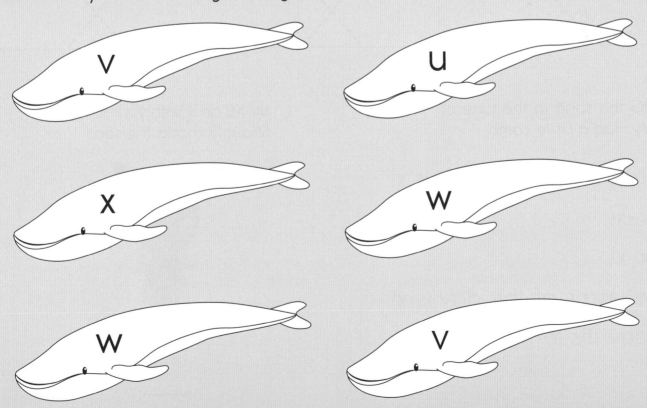

The Letter x

Trace & Sing

Lowercase **x** matches uppercase **X**. TRACE the letter **x**.
START at the green arrow labeled with a number 1.

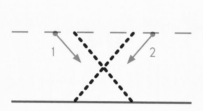

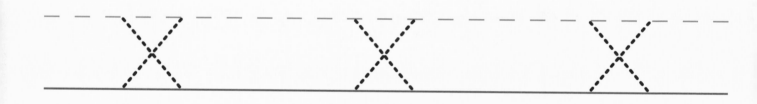

SING this song to the tune of
Mary Had a Little Lamb.

The letter of the day is **x**!

x-x-x!

x-x-x!

The letter of the day is **x**!

Today it's letter **x**!

MAKE an **x** with your arms.
Shout "X marks the spot!"

110

Practice the Letter x

CIRCLE every x in the box. CROSS OUT every v.

y	k	x	v
w	x	v	y
x	v	k	x

DRAW a line to connect each pair of uppercase and lowercase letters.

b F m X u i

H q

I B

x f Q h M U

Trace & Sing

Lowercase y matches uppercase Y. TRACE the letter y.
START at the green arrow labeled with a number 1.

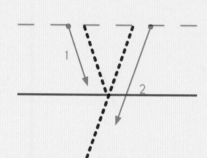

SING this song to the tune of
Jingle Bells.

MAKE a y using two socks
(one small and one big).

Letter y! Letter y!

Hello, letter y!

We meet a letter every day.

Today it's letter y!

[Shout] y!

Alphabet Art

COLOR the **y** spaces green. COLOR the **x** spaces pink. Then COLOR the **w** spaces brown.

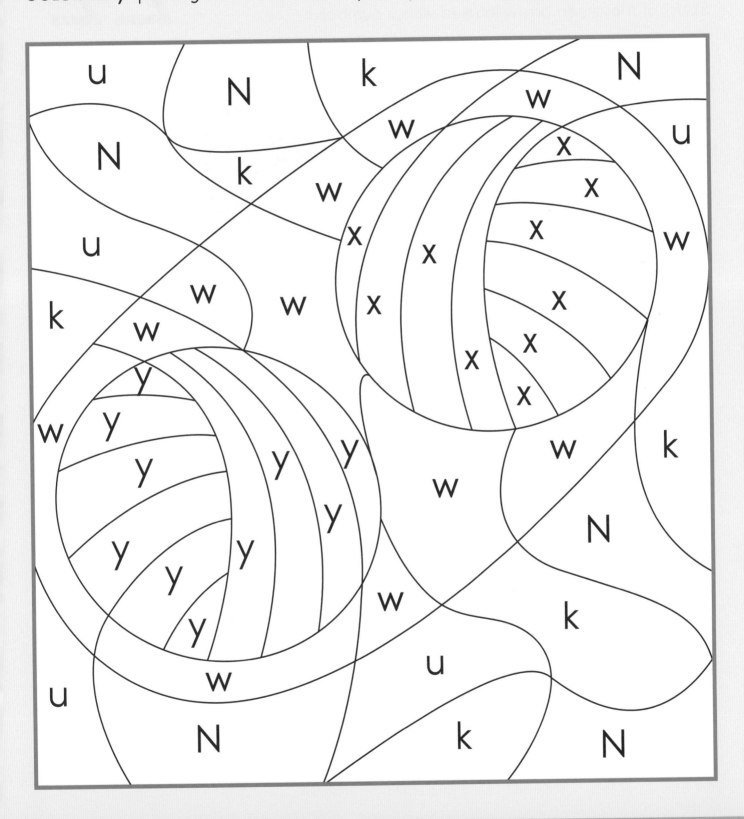

Zz

Trace & Sing

Lowercase **z** matches uppercase **Z**. TRACE the letter **z**.
START at the green arrow labeled with a number 1.

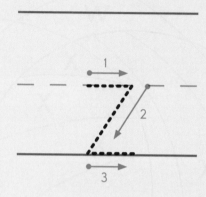

SING this song to the tune of
Mary Had a Little Lamb.

MAKE a **z** with three strips of
paper (all the same size).

The letter of the day is **z**!

z-z-z!

z-z-z!

The letter of the day is **z**!

Today it's letter **z**!

Match Maker

SING the alphabet song. FOLLOW ALONG with the alphabet. DRAW a line to connect each letter in the box to its place in the alphabet.

z   l   d   q   w

a b c ☐ e f g h i

j k ☐ m n o p ☐ r

s t u v ☐ x y ☐

Connect the Dots

DRAW a line to connect the dots in order from **a** to **z**.

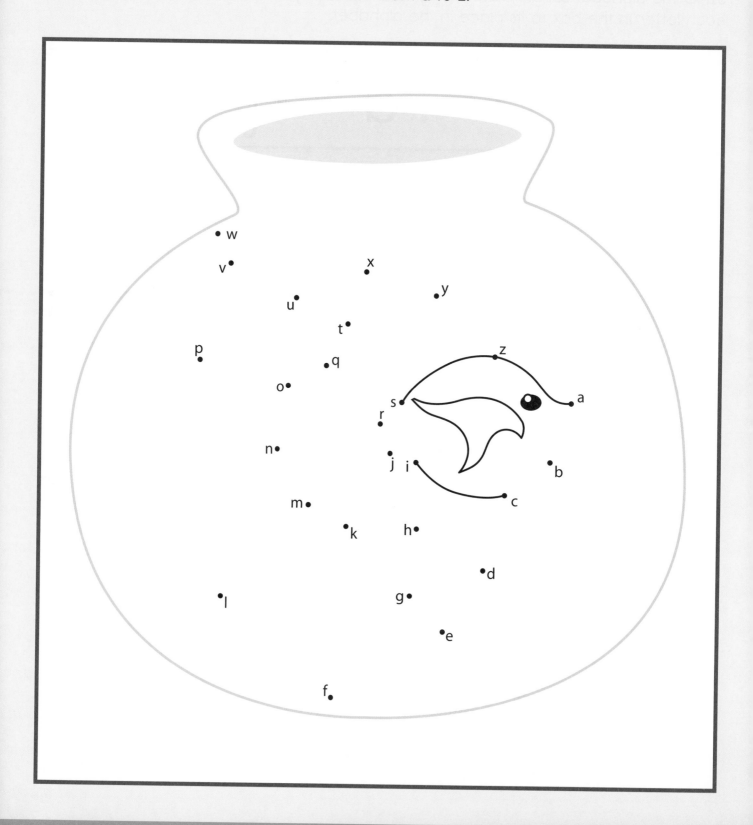

Review

Trace & Sing

TRACE the alphabet, SING the alphabet song as you trace.

NOTE: This activity continues on pages 118 and 119.

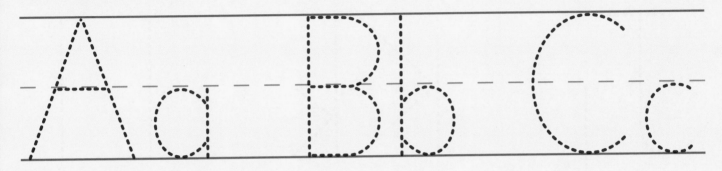

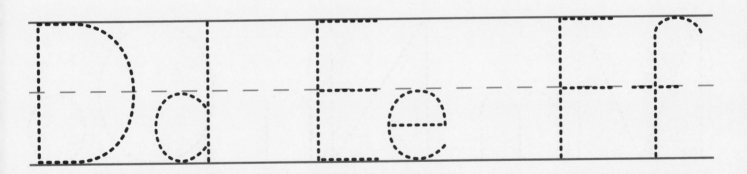

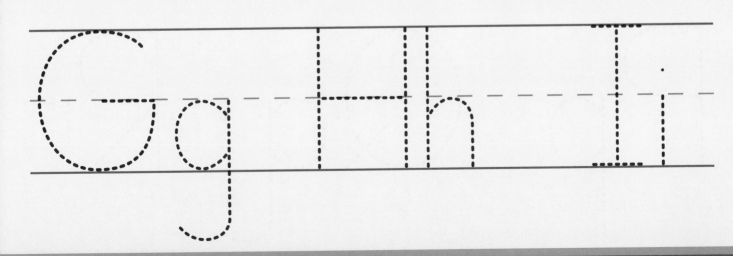

Trace & Sing

CONTINUE tracing the alphabet. SING the alphabet song as you trace.

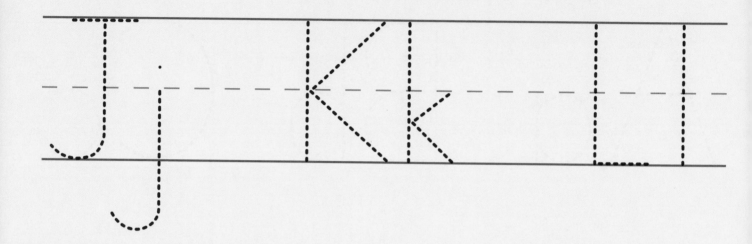

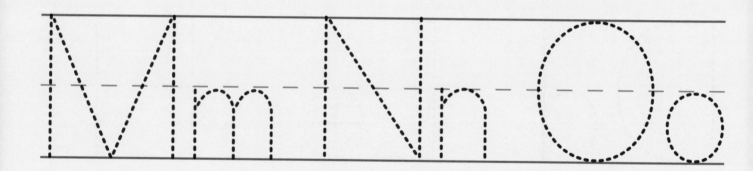

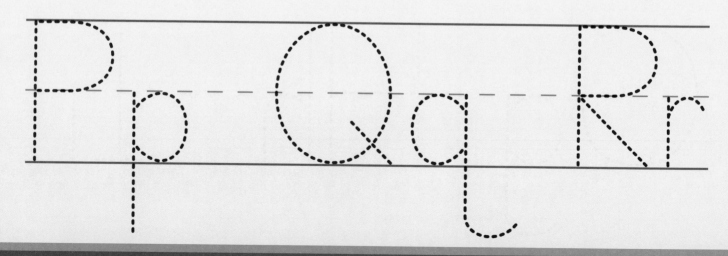

Ss Tt Uu

Vv Ww

Xx Yy Zz

Answers

Page 3

Page 5

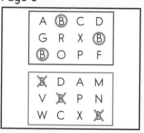

Page 7

Page 9

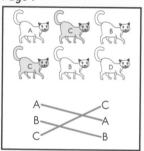

Page 11

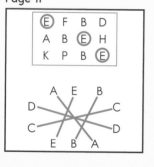

Page 13

Page 15

Page 16

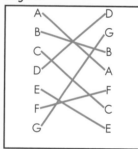

Page 17

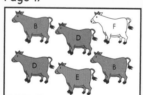

Page 19

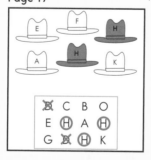

Page 21

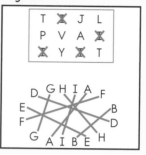

Page 23

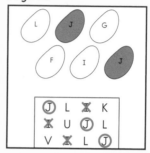

Page 25

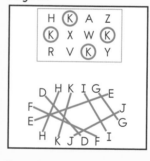

Page 27

Page 29

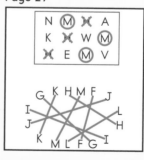

Page 31

Page 33

Page 35

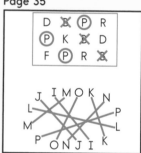

Page 36

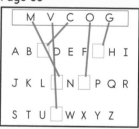

Page 39

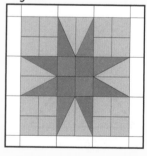

Answers

Page 41

Page 43
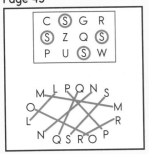

Page 45

Page 47
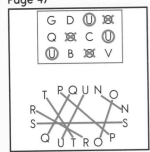

Page 49

Page 51
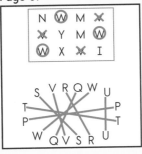

Page 53

Page 55
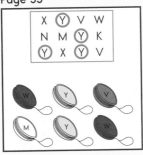

Page 57

Page 58
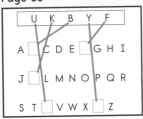

Page 59

Page 61
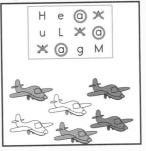

Page 63

Page 65
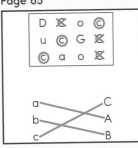

Page 67
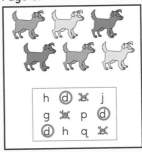

Page 69
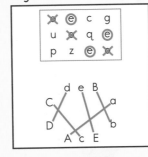

Page 71
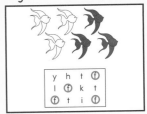

Page 73

Page 74
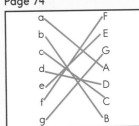

Page 75

Page 77
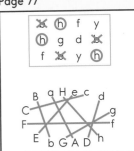

Page 79
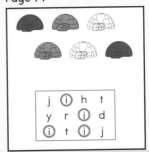

Answers

Page 81
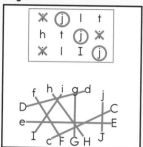

Page 91
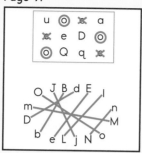

Page 101

Page 111
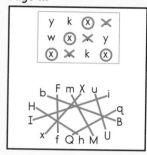

Page 83

Page 93
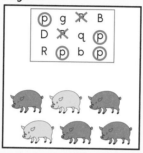

Page 103
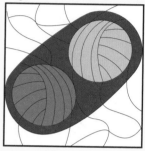

Page 113
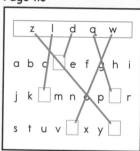

Page 85

Page 95
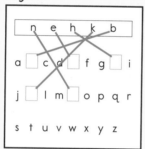

Page 105

Page 115

Page 87
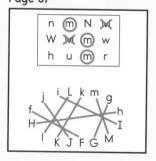

Page 97
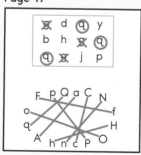

Page 107
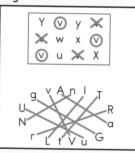

Page 116
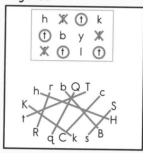

Page 89
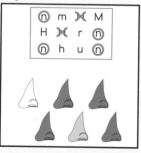

Page 99

Page 109